SELF-CARE AFFIRMATIONS FOR BLACK WOMEN

Inspiring Affirmations to Nurture the Strong Black Woman Within

SIMONE BELLO

from various sources. Please consult a licensed professional before attempting any techniques outlined in this book.
By reading this document, the reader agrees that under no circumstances is the author responsible for any losses, direct or indirect, that are incurred as a result of the use of the information contained within this document, including, but not limited to, errors, omissions, or inaccuracies.

CONTENTS

Chapter 1: Embracing Self-Love 6

Chapter 2: Cultivating Inner Strength 17

Chapter 3: Nurturing Emotional Well Being 28

Chapter 4: Building Healthy Relationships 39

Chapter 5: Balancing Personal and Professional Life 54

Afterword 69

Introduction

Welcome to "Self-Care Affirmations for Black Women," a book dedicated to empowering and uplifting Black women on their journey towards self-care and self-love. In a world that often overlooks our unique experiences and struggles, we must prioritize our well-being and nurture ourselves in every way possible.

Self-care is more than just a buzzword; it is a revolutionary act of self-preservation and self-empowerment. As Black women, we face intersecting challenges, including systemic racism, gender bias, and societal expectations. Our strength and resilience are undeniable, but it is crucial to recognize that we deserve care, compassion, and time to replenish our spirits.

This book is designed to be a sanctuary—a safe space where you can find solace, inspiration, and practical tools to navigate the complexities of life. Through the power of affirmations, we will harness the strength of our words and thoughts to transform our mindset, enhance our self-worth, and embrace the beauty of self-care.

Each chapter will delve into different aspects of self-care, offering a range of affirmations tailored specifically to our experiences as Black women. Together, we will explore the importance of self-love, inner strength, emotional well-being, building healthy relationships, and finding balance in our personal and professional lives.

As you immerse yourself in these pages, allow the affirmations to resonate with your soul. They will serve as gentle reminders of your worth, reminding you that you are deserving of love, joy, and abundance. Embrace these affirmations, integrate them into your daily routine, and witness the transformative power they hold.

Remember, self-care is a radical act of self-preservation, and by prioritizing our well-being, we are nurturing the seeds of change and empowerment within ourselves. Together, we will create a future where Black women thrive, where our needs and dreams are valued, and where self-care is seen as a birthright rather than a luxury.

It is my honor to guide you on this journey of self-care, and I invite you to embark on this transformative path with an open heart and a commitment to honoring yourself. Let these affirmations be a source of strength, inspiration, and unwavering support as you reclaim your power and embrace the fullness of who you are.

With love and solidarity,
Simone Bello

1

Embracing Self-Love

In a world that often bombards us with unrealistic standards of beauty and constantly tells us we are not enough, it becomes crucial for Black women to cultivate a deep sense of self-love. Embracing self-love is not only an act of defiance against societal norms, but it is also a transformative practice that can positively impact every aspect of our lives.

My Blackness is beautiful, and I celebrate the richness of my heritage.

I honor and respect my body, embracing its unique shape and size.

I release comparison and embrace my own journey with love and compassion.

I deserve to prioritize my well-being and make self-care a non-negotiable part of my life.

My voice and opinions are valuable, and I confidently express myself.

I am deserving of happiness, joy, and fulfillment in all areas of my life.

I forgive myself for past mistakes and embrace my journey of growth and self-discovery.

I surround myself with people who uplift and support me in my self-love journey.

I radiate love and compassion, both towards myself and others.

I am deserving of love and happiness.

My worthiness is not defined by external validation.

I radiate beauty from within, and it shines through me.

I embrace my flaws as unique expressions of my individuality.

I love and accept myself unconditionally.

I am proud of my heritage and the strength it represents.

My Blackness is a source of power, grace, and resilience.

I am confident in my own skin and celebrate my unique beauty.

I release the need to conform to societal beauty standards.

I choose to nourish my body with love and respect.

I am grateful for the vessel that carries my spirit and allows me to experience life.

I speak kindly to myself and replace self-criticism with self-compassion.

I am whole and complete, just as I am.

I am deserving of all the love and joy that life has to offer.

I release comparison and honor my own journey.

I am worthy of success, abundance, and fulfillment.

I let go of toxic relationships that do not serve my growth and well-being.

I set healthy boundaries that protect my energy and self-worth.

I trust my intuition to guide me towards what is best for me.

I am deserving of respect, love, and kindness from others.

I forgive myself for past mistakes and embrace the lessons they have taught me.

I am resilient and capable of overcoming any challenge.

I am a magnet for positive experiences and loving relationships.

I attract opportunities that align with my highest good.

I honor my emotions and allow myself to feel deeply.

I am worthy of pursuing my dreams and achieving my goals.

I am a masterpiece, a work of art, and I appreciate my own unique beauty.

I celebrate my strengths and use them to uplift myself and others.

I choose self-care as an act of self-love and nourishment.

I am a vessel of love, and I share it generously with the world.

I acknowledge and honor my needs, giving myself permission to prioritize self-care.

I release the need to seek validation from others; my validation comes from within.

I am grateful for my journey and the growth it has
brought me.

I am deserving of all the good that flows into my
life.

I embrace my voice and express my thoughts
and opinions with confidence.

I am a beacon of love, light, and positivity.

I am proud of the person I am becoming.

I attract supportive and nurturing relationships
into my life.

I am open to receiving love, kindness, and
abundance from the universe.

I am resilient and can handle anything that
comes my way.

I honor my past and use it as a stepping stone
towards a brighter future.

2

Cultivating Inner Strength

In a world that can often be challenging and unpredictable, cultivating inner strength becomes a powerful tool for Black women to navigate the ups and downs of life with resilience and grace. Inner strength is not about suppressing emotions or putting on a facade of invincibility; rather, it is about tapping into our inherent power, harnessing our resilience, and embracing the core of who we are.

I am resilient and capable of overcoming any obstacle.

I trust in my ability to handle whatever comes my way.

I embrace challenges as opportunities for growth and learning.

My past experiences have equipped me with strength and wisdom.

I am the author of my own story and have the power to shape my destiny.

I face adversity with courage, knowing that I am stronger than any circumstance.

I let go of fear and step into my power.

I believe in myself and my abilities.

I stand tall and confident in my truth.

I am rooted in resilience, grace, and unwavering determination.

I am resilient, and I bounce back from challenges stronger than before.

I have the inner strength to overcome any obstacle in my path.

My inner strength grows with every challenge I face.

I trust in my ability to navigate life's uncertainties with grace and resilience.

I am grounded in my inner power and strength.

I embrace discomfort as an opportunity for
growth and transformation.

I am not defined by my past; I am empowered by
the strength it has given me.

I release the need for external validation and find
strength within myself.

I face fear with courage and take bold steps
towards my goals.

My inner strength allows me to persevere
through difficult times.

I trust my intuition to guide me towards the right
path.

I am capable, confident, and resilient in the face
of adversity.

I let go of what I cannot control and focus on
what I can.
I am a force to be reckoned with, capable of
achieving greatness.
I tap into my inner wisdom and make decisions
with clarity and confidence.

I embrace change and adapt to new circumstances with strength and resilience.

I am the master of my thoughts, and I choose positivity and resilience.

I draw strength from my past victories, knowing that I can overcome anything.

I embrace challenges as opportunities for growth and personal development.

I am in control of my responses and choose resilience in the face of adversity.

I believe in my abilities and trust that I have what it takes to succeed.

I am capable of finding solutions to any problem that comes my way.

I release self-doubt and step into my power with confidence.

I am worthy of love, respect, and success, and I attract these into my life.

I rise above negativity and embrace positivity and inner strength.

I am resilient in the face of criticism, knowing my worth and value.

I face challenges head-on, knowing they are opportunities for growth.

I am deserving of all the blessings and abundance that life has to offer.

I am a warrior, and I navigate life's battles with strength and grace.

I am grateful for the lessons learned through adversity, as they have made me stronger.

I trust the journey, knowing that every experience serves a purpose in my growth.

I release the need for perfection and embrace my authentic self with love and acceptance.

I draw strength from within, knowing that my power is limitless.

I am flexible and adaptable, capable of navigating life's twists and turns.

I am resilient in the face of setbacks, and I use them as stepping stones to success.

I am a source of inspiration and strength to those around me.

I tap into my inner courage and take bold action towards my dreams.

I am unshakeable in my faith and belief in myself.

I am resourceful, and I find creative solutions to challenges.

I release the need for control and trust in the greater plan unfolding for me.

I believe in my abilities and trust that I have what it takes to succeed.

3

Nurturing Emotional Well Being

Emotional well-being is a vital aspect of self-care for Black women. It involves understanding, acknowledging, and nurturing our emotions in a way that promotes balance, resilience, and overall mental health. By prioritizing our emotional well-being, we empower ourselves to navigate the complexities of life with greater clarity, compassion, and self-awareness.

I honor and acknowledge my emotions with compassion and understanding.

I create space for my emotions to be felt and expressed without judgment.

I cultivate a healthy relationship with my emotions, allowing them to guide me towards healing and growth.

I am deserving of emotional support and seek it
when needed.

I prioritize self-care practices that nourish and
restore my emotional well-being.

I release the need to suppress or deny my
emotions and embrace the wisdom they hold.

I choose to respond to challenging situations with
grace and emotional resilience.

I create healthy boundaries that protect my
emotional well-being.

I am in control of my emotional state, and I
choose to cultivate positivity and peace.

I am gentle with myself during times of emotional
difficulty, knowing that healing takes time.

I embrace and honor all of my emotions.

I am allowed to feel a range of emotions, and
each one serves a purpose.

I am worthy of love, understanding, and
compassion.

My emotions guide me towards self-discovery and growth.

I give myself permission to let go of emotions that no longer serve me.

I am resilient and capable of navigating through emotional challenges.

My emotions are valid, and I trust my inner wisdom.

I release any guilt or shame associated with expressing my emotions.

I create space for healing and emotional restoration in my life.

I am in control of how I respond to and process my emotions.

I am gentle with myself during times of emotional difficulty.

I embrace vulnerability as a gateway to emotional authenticity and connection.

I deserve to prioritize my emotional well-being.

I attract and cultivate relationships that support
my emotional growth and well-being.

I let go of the need for external validation and
find validation within myself.

I am resilient and capable of bouncing back from
emotional setbacks.

My emotions are a valuable source of information
and guidance.

I give myself permission to seek support and ask
for help when needed.

I create healthy boundaries that protect my
emotional well-being.

I am deserving of love, care, and kindness from
myself and others.

I release expectations and embrace the flow of
my emotions.

I am open to learning from my emotions and
using them as tools for personal growth.

I cultivate self-awareness and actively explore the root causes of my emotions.

I release the need to control or suppress my emotions and allow them to flow naturally.

I trust my intuition to guide me towards emotional well-being.

I am resilient, and I bounce back from emotional challenges with grace and strength.

I choose to focus on the present moment and let go of past emotional burdens.

I am worthy of experiencing joy, peace, and emotional fulfillment.

I celebrate my emotional victories, no matter how small.

I let go of comparison and embrace my unique emotional journey.

I nourish my emotional well-being through self-care practices that align with my needs.

I release any negative beliefs I have about my emotions and embrace their transformative power.

I am allowed to prioritize my emotional well-being without guilt or explanation.

I trust myself to make choices that honor my emotional needs and values.

I am connected to a deep well of inner strength and resilience.

I forgive myself for any past emotional mistakes and choose to move forward with compassion.

I let go of perfectionism and embrace the beauty of my imperfect emotional journey.

I release the need to judge or criticize my emotions and instead approach them with curiosity and acceptance.

I am capable of finding peace and balance amidst life's emotional ups and downs.

I am deserving of a life filled with emotional well-being, joy, and fulfillment.

My emotions are a valuable source of information
and guidance.

4

Building Healthy Relationships

Building healthy relationships is essential for our overall well-being as Black women. These relationships provide us with support, love, and a sense of belonging. They contribute to our emotional, mental, and even physical health. By cultivating healthy relationships, we create a nurturing and empowering network of individuals who uplift and inspire us on our journey of self-care and personal growth.

Understanding Healthy Relationships:

Respect: Healthy relationships are built on a foundation of mutual respect, where each person's boundaries, opinions, and individuality are valued and honored.

Communication: Effective communication is key to maintaining healthy relationships. It involves active listening, expressing oneself honestly and respectfully, and working together to resolve conflicts.

Trust: Trust is the cornerstone of healthy relationships. It requires reliability, honesty, and consistency in words and actions. Trust allows us to feel safe and secure within our relationships.

Boundaries: Setting and respecting boundaries is essential for maintaining healthy relationships. Boundaries define what is acceptable and what is not, ensuring that our needs, values, and limits are honored.

Support: Healthy relationships provide emotional support, encouragement, and validation. They involve being there for each other during both triumphs and challenges, and fostering an environment where growth and well-being are nurtured.

Building Healthy Relationships:

Self-Awareness: Start by developing self-awareness, understanding your own needs, values, and boundaries. This awareness will guide you in forming relationships that align with who you are.

Choosing Healthy Partnerships: Select relationships that prioritize mutual respect, open communication, and shared values. Surround yourself with individuals who uplift and support your well-being.

Active Listening: Practice active listening by giving your full attention to others, seeking to understand their perspective, and responding with empathy and respect.

Effective Communication: Enhance your communication skills by expressing your thoughts, feelings, and needs clearly and assertively. Practice active problem-solving and avoid destructive communication patterns, such as blame or defensiveness.

Honoring Boundaries: Respect both your own boundaries and those of others. Communicate your boundaries clearly and be mindful of not crossing others' boundaries. This creates a foundation of trust and respect in relationships.

Nurturing Trust: Build trust through consistency, honesty, and reliability. Be accountable for your actions and words, and demonstrate integrity in your interactions.

Cultivating Empathy: Develop empathy by seeking to understand others' perspectives, experiences, and emotions. Empathy allows for deeper connection and fosters a sense of compassion within relationships.

Conflict Resolution: Learn constructive ways to manage conflicts and disagreements. Practice active listening, finding common ground, and working towards solutions that benefit both parties.

Emotional Support: Be a source of emotional support for others and seek support when needed. Create an environment where vulnerability is encouraged and where individuals can openly express their feelings without judgment.

Cultivating Equality and Equity: Foster relationships based on equality, where power dynamics are balanced and decision-making is shared. Advocate for fairness and inclusivity within your relationships.

Healthy Communication Technology Use: Be mindful of how technology impacts your relationships. Set boundaries around screen time, prioritize face-to-face interactions, and use technology to enhance, rather than replace, meaningful connections.

Self-Care in Relationships: Remember to prioritize your own self-care while building healthy relationships. Take time for activities that recharge you, set aside alone time, and honor your personal well-being.

I attract and cultivate healthy, supportive relationships in my life.

I am deserving of respectful and loving connections in all areas of my life.

I communicate my needs and boundaries with clarity and confidence.

I surround myself with individuals who uplift and inspire me.

I am a good listener, providing space for others to share their thoughts and emotions.

I choose relationships that align with my values and contribute positively to my well-being.

I am worthy of love, understanding, and compassion within my relationships.

I nurture trust and honesty within my connections, fostering deep and meaningful bonds.

I communicate effectively and assertively, expressing my thoughts and emotions with clarity

I am open to learning and growing within my relationships, embracing new perspectives and experiences.

I celebrate diversity within my relationships, appreciating the richness that different backgrounds and perspectives bring.

I set healthy boundaries that protect my well-being and honor my needs and values.

I attract relationships that promote mutual respect, equality, and shared decision-making.

I am grateful for the supportive individuals in my life who contribute positively to my well-being.

I choose relationships that encourage my personal growth, nurturing my journey of self-discovery.

I am a source of empathy and understanding, providing emotional support to those I care about.

I create a nurturing and loving environment within my relationships, fostering a sense of safety and acceptance.

I choose to resolve conflicts with compassion and understanding, seeking resolutions that benefit all parties involved.

I celebrate the joys and successes of my loved ones, encouraging their growth and happiness.

I am committed to building and maintaining healthy relationships that bring joy, fulfillment, and love into my life.

I attract people who appreciate and value me for who I am.

I radiate love and kindness, attracting loving and kind individuals into my life.

I am a magnet for positive and nurturing relationships.

I am open-hearted and receptive to the love and connection that comes my way.

I deserve relationships that bring out the best in me and inspire my growth.

I choose to let go of toxic relationships and create space for healthy connections.

I am deserving of love, respect, and reciprocity in my relationships.

I communicate my needs and desires with clarity and confidence.

I am skilled at resolving conflicts peacefully and finding win-win solutions.

I cultivate deep and meaningful connections with those who uplift and support me.

I am committed to being present and fully engaged in my relationships.

I attract friends who are loyal, trustworthy, and supportive.

I am surrounded by people who believe in my dreams and encourage my success.

I embrace vulnerability in my relationships, allowing for deeper intimacy and connection.

I release the need to control and instead trust in the natural flow of my relationships.

I attract partners who cherish and respect me.

I communicate my boundaries with ease and assertiveness.

I choose relationships that nurture my well-being and contribute positively to my life.

I am a source of inspiration and encouragement for my loved ones.

I attract and maintain balanced and harmonious relationships.

I am worthy of receiving love and affection in my relationships.

I create space for open and honest communication within my relationships.

I am a supportive and understanding friend, partner, and family member.

I release any fear or insecurity that hinders my ability to form healthy connections.

I am deserving of healthy and loving relationships in every area of my life.

I attract individuals who appreciate my unique qualities and celebrate my successes.

I am surrounded by people who uplift and inspire me to be my best self.

I am a magnet for positive, like-minded individuals who share my values and aspirations.

I choose relationships that empower me to grow and evolve into my highest potential.

I trust my intuition to guide me towards relationships that serve my highest good.

I am surrounded by individuals who respect and support my personal boundaries.

I attract relationships that are filled with joy, laughter, and genuine connection.

I am open to giving and receiving love in all its forms.
I am a valuable and cherished presence in the lives of those I care about.

I release any past hurts or resentments and open myself to new, healthy relationships.

I communicate my boundaries with ease and assertiveness.

5

Balancing Personal and Professional Life

Balancing personal and professional life is a crucial aspect of self-care for Black women. It involves finding harmony between our personal responsibilities, relationships, and professional pursuits. Striking this balance empowers us to lead fulfilling lives, nurture our well-being, and thrive in all areas of our existence. In this chapter, we will explore strategies and practices to help you achieve a harmonious integration of your personal and professional life.

Understanding the Importance of Balance:

Well-being: Balancing personal and professional life is essential for maintaining our physical, mental, and emotional well-being. It allows us to avoid burnout and sustain our energy and enthusiasm.

Fulfillment: Achieving balance enables us to pursue our personal passions and goals, leading to a greater sense of fulfillment and purpose in life.

Relationships: Balancing personal and professional life ensures that we allocate time and attention to nurture our relationships, fostering deeper connections with loved ones.

Self-Care: Achieving balance allows us to prioritize self-care, ensuring that we attend to our physical and mental health needs.

Strategies for Balancing Personal and Professional Life:

Prioritization: Clarify your values and priorities to identify what truly matters to you. This helps you allocate time and energy to activities and relationships that align with your personal and professional goals.

Boundaries: Set clear boundaries between your personal and professional life. Establish designated times for work, relaxation, family time, and self-care. Communicate these boundaries to others and enforce them with discipline.

Time Management: Adopt effective time management techniques to optimize your productivity and create space for personal and professional activities. Prioritize tasks, delegate when possible, and avoid overcommitting yourself.

Self-Care Rituals: Incorporate regular self-care rituals into your daily routine. Engage in activities that nourish your mind, body, and soul, such as exercise, meditation, journaling, or pursuing hobbies.

Support System: Seek support from friends, family, or mentors who understand the importance of work-life balance. Surround yourself with individuals who encourage and uplift you in maintaining equilibrium.

Flexibility: Embrace flexibility in managing your personal and professional life. Allow room for adjustments and adaptability, recognizing that balance may look different at different stages of life.

Delegation and Outsourcing: Delegate tasks and responsibilities whenever possible. Consider outsourcing certain tasks to lighten your load and create more time for personal activities.

Mindfulness: Practice mindfulness to stay present and focused on the task at hand. This enhances your efficiency, reduces stress, and allows you to fully engage in both personal and professional activities.

Communication: Foster open and honest communication with your employer, colleagues, and loved ones about your boundaries, needs, and commitments. Advocate for work-life balance and create a supportive environment.

Letting Go of Perfectionism: Release the need for perfectionism and embrace the concept of "good enough." Understand that balance requires finding realistic and sustainable solutions, rather than striving for unattainable ideals.

Integration: Seek opportunities to integrate personal and professional activities whenever possible. For example, consider engaging in exercise or self-reflection during your lunch breaks.

Celebrate Achievements: Celebrate your achievements, both personal and professional. Acknowledge your successes and reward yourself for your efforts, reinforcing the importance of balance and self-care.

I effortlessly create a harmonious balance between my personal and professional life.

I prioritize self-care and well-being in both my personal and professional endeavors.

I establish and maintain healthy boundaries that honor my personal and professional needs.

I am capable of achieving success

I am in control of my time and effectively manage my personal and professional commitments.

I embrace flexibility and adaptability in balancing my personal and professional life.

I release the need for perfectionism and embrace progress over perfection.

I communicate my needs and boundaries with confidence and clarity.

I create a supportive network that understands and respects my pursuit of work-life balance.

I prioritize quality time with my loved ones, fostering deeper connections and nurturing relationships.

I make time for self-care and prioritize my physical, mental, and emotional well-being.

I delegate tasks and ask for help when needed, recognizing that I don't have to do everything alone.

I celebrate my achievements, big and small, in both my personal and professional life.

I trust in my ability to achieve balance and create a fulfilling life.

I am deserving of a harmonious and fulfilling personal and professional life.

I find joy and satisfaction in both my personal and professional pursuits.

I am capable of successfully managing multiple areas of my life with grace and ease.

I am present and fully engaged in each moment, whether it's personal or professional.

I release guilt and embrace the concept of self-care and balance.

I trust my intuition to guide me in making decisions that support my work-life balance.

I attract opportunities that align with my values and contribute to my overall well-being.

I am grateful for the abundance of time and resources to create balance in my life.

I create harmony by aligning my personal and professional goals.

I find joy in the journey of balancing my personal and professional life.

I am resilient in the face of challenges, maintaining balance and perspective.

I am in tune with my needs and make self-care a non-negotiable priority.

I am a role model for others, demonstrating the importance of work-life balance.

I release the need to constantly hustle and allow myself time for rest and rejuvenation.

I attract opportunities for growth and success that honor my need for balance.

I am in control of my schedule and create time for activities that bring me joy and fulfillment.

I embrace a holistic approach to life, honoring the interconnectedness of personal and professional aspects.

I release comparison and focus on my unique journey to create balance in my life.

I set realistic goals and celebrate progress along the way.

I maintain harmony by practicing self-reflection and adjusting as needed.

I trust that by nurturing both my personal and professional life, I can achieve greater overall success.

I find peace in embracing imperfections and learning from life's challenges.

I attract supportive and understanding individuals who respect and honor my need for balance.

I am in control of my time and use it wisely to create a fulfilling and balanced life.

I am confident in my ability to create boundaries that allow me to prioritize my well-being.

I trust that my commitment to work-life balance will lead to greater fulfillment and happiness.

I am worthy of a life filled with balance, harmony, and fulfillment.

I create a schedule that allows me to prioritize both my personal and professional needs.

I release any guilt or shame associated with taking time for myself and pursuing my passions.

I find creative ways to blend my personal and professional responsibilities to create synergy and efficiency.

I honor my physical and mental well-being by prioritizing self-care and setting aside time for rest and rejuvenation.

I gracefully navigate transitions between work and personal life, maintaining a sense of balance and calm.

I release the need to constantly be busy and embrace the importance of creating space for relaxation and leisure.

I communicate my boundaries with confidence and assertiveness, ensuring that my personal time is respected.

I attract supportive mentors and colleagues who understand and encourage the importance of work-life balance.

I let go of the pressure to "do it all" and instead focus on doing what truly matters to me.

I celebrate my achievements in both my personal and professional life, acknowledging the progress I have made.

I trust in divine timing, knowing that everything will fall into place when I prioritize balance and well-being.

I am grateful for the opportunities that come my way, knowing that they contribute to my overall fulfillment and happiness.

I embrace self-reflection as a tool for assessing and adjusting my work-life balance to ensure harmony and satisfaction.

I release the need for external validation and find fulfillment in honoring my personal values and desires.

Sustaining Faith: Dealing with Doubt and Uncertainty

Faith is often accompanied by periods of doubt and uncertainty, and learning to navigate these experiences is a critical aspect of the faith journey for Black women. Doubt is not the opposite of faith; rather, it can serve as a catalyst for deeper understanding and growth. Engaging with doubt and uncertainty can lead to a more mature, resilient faith that can weather life's storms.

Navigating these challenging periods involves being honest about doubts, seeking guidance and support from trusted individuals or communities, and continuing to engage with spiritual practices. Embracing the journey through doubt and uncertainty can strengthen Black women's faith, deepening their trust in God's faithfulness and love.

The Intersection of Faith and Feminism

The intersection of faith and feminism is a crucial area of exploration for Black women. Feminist perspectives can inform their understanding of faith, offering insights into issues of equality, justice, and dignity within religious contexts. These perspectives can challenge patriarchal structures and interpretations, paving the way for a more inclusive and equitable faith experience.

At the same time, faith can inform and enrich their feminism, providing a spiritual foundation for their advocacy for gender equality. Faith-based feminism acknowledges the inherent dignity and worth of all individuals, grounded in the belief in a loving, just God. Exploring this intersection can empower Black women to advocate for gender equality within their faith communities and broader society.

Faith and Leadership: Guiding Others on the Journey

Many Black women are called to leadership roles within their faith communities, serving as pastors, ministers, counselors, or group leaders. These leadership roles offer opportunities to guide, support, and inspire others on their faith journeys.

Faith leadership involves embodying the values of their faith, offering spiritual guidance, and fostering a supportive, inclusive community. It's about empowering others to grow in their faith, navigate challenges, and live out their beliefs. For Black women, faith leadership can be a powerful way to serve their communities, contribute to the growth of their faith communities, and impact the lives of others in meaningful ways.

Bridging Faith and Culture: Nurturing a Culturally-Relevant Faith

Bridging faith and culture involves integrating cultural experiences and heritage into faith practices and understanding. For Black women, a culturally-relevant faith acknowledges and celebrates their cultural heritage while exploring how it interacts with their faith.

This approach to faith enables Black women to see their cultural experiences reflected in their faith journey. It provides space for cultural expressions of worship, interpretation of scriptures through the lens of their cultural experiences, and the addressing of culturally-specific issues within a faith context. Bridging faith and culture allows Black women to experience a faith that is both personally relevant and deeply rooted in their cultural identity.

A Creative Expression: Art, Music, and Faith

The intersection of art, music, and faith offers a rich platform for Black women to express their spirituality. Music, particularly gospel and spirituals, has historically played a significant role in the faith practices of Black communities. These creative outlets allow for the expression of faith in ways that words alone may not capture, invoking emotion and fostering connection.

Artistic expressions, be it through painting, dance, poetry, or other forms, can serve as a means to communicate faith experiences, question beliefs, and explore spiritual themes. By engaging with art and music, Black women can experience a deeper understanding of their faith, a heightened sense of connection with the divine, and a unique medium for sharing their faith with others.

Faith in the Face of Injustice: Spiritual Activism

For Black women, faith is not just a personal spiritual experience, but often also a source of strength in the face of social injustice. Spiritual activism is about using faith as a driving force for advocating for social change and justice.

From the civil rights movements to modern struggles against systemic racism, Black women have historically leaned into their faith as a source of resilience, inspiration, and mobilization. In this way, their faith is not just about personal salvation or spiritual growth, but also about striving for justice, equality, and a better world.

Nurturing Faith in the Family: Faith Traditions and Practices

Family plays a central role in nurturing and sustaining faith for many Black women. Family traditions, practices, and discussions around faith can significantly shape an individual's spiritual journey. The home can serve as a critical space for learning about faith, practicing spiritual disciplines, and fostering a sense of religious identity.

By sharing faith experiences and traditions within the family, Black women can pass their faith to the next generation, shaping their children's spiritual formation and understanding of God. These faith experiences in the family context create a meaningful, personal, and enduring foundation for faith.

Faith and Healing: Finding Restoration in Faith

Faith plays a significant role in the healing process for many Black women. In the face of personal or communal trauma, faith can offer comfort, hope, and a sense of divine companionship. It can be a source of strength and resilience, providing a spiritual framework for understanding and processing pain.

Through faith, Black women can find a path towards healing and restoration. Faith practices such as prayer, meditation, communal worship, and scripture reading can facilitate emotional healing, promote peace of mind, and foster spiritual growth amidst difficulties. This intersection between faith and healing illustrates the restorative power of faith in the lives of Black women.

Faith and Empowerment: Finding Strength in Spirituality

For many Black women, faith is not just a set of beliefs but a source of empowerment and resilience. This spiritual strength enables them to face challenges, overcome obstacles, and strive towards their goals. Empowerment through faith can take many forms, including the courage to stand up against injustice, the determination to overcome personal trials, or the conviction to pursue one's aspirations.

Faith empowers Black women by affirming their inherent worth, their ability to effect change, and their capacity for resilience in the face of adversity. By exploring the intersection between faith and empowerment, Black women can discover the transformative power of faith to inspire, motivate, and strengthen.

The Role of Faith in Community Building

Faith plays a significant role in building and sustaining communities. Black women often take active roles in their religious communities, fostering unity, mutual support, and a collective identity. These communities provide a space for shared worship, learning, service, and fellowship.

Through active participation in faith-based communities, Black women can forge deep and meaningful connections with others. They can contribute to their communities through service, share their wisdom and experiences, and gain support and encouragement for their faith journey. This active community engagement not only strengthens the faith of the individual but also contributes to a vibrant and resilient faith community.

The Influence of Historical Figures: Faith and Role Models

Historical figures and role models can greatly influence the faith journey of Black women. Figures such as Sojourner Truth, Harriet Tubman, and many others have demonstrated a deep and resilient faith in the face of immense adversity. Their stories provide inspiration and offer valuable lessons about the power of faith.

Drawing on the wisdom, courage, and faith of these role models, Black women can navigate their own faith journeys with greater understanding and confidence. These historical figures serve as powerful reminders of the strength and resilience that faith can foster.

The Power of Storytelling in Faith

Storytelling is a powerful tool in exploring and sharing faith. Sharing personal faith stories allows Black women to reflect on their spiritual journeys, articulate their experiences, and connect with others on a deeper level. These stories can offer encouragement, wisdom, and hope, fostering a sense of shared experience and mutual understanding within the faith community.

Through storytelling, Black women can explore the complexities of their faith, celebrate their growth, and express their hopes and doubts. This practice not only enriches their personal faith experience but also contributes to a vibrant and supportive faith community.

Faith and Intersectionality: The Layered Experiences of Faith

Intersectionality provides a framework for understanding the layered experiences of Black women in faith. The concept of intersectionality recognizes that individuals can experience multiple forms of oppression based on their race, gender, class, or other social identities. For Black women, their experiences of faith are often influenced by their identities as Black, as women, and potentially other factors such as socioeconomic status, education, and age.

Intersectionality in faith means acknowledging and addressing the specific challenges and experiences that Black women face. This can lead to a deeper understanding of their faith journeys, fostering a more inclusive and empathetic faith community. Recognizing and addressing intersectionality can help to ensure that faith practices and communities are welcoming, affirming, and supportive of Black women in all their diversity.

Faith and Mental Health: Spiritual Support for Wellbeing

Mental health is a crucial aspect of overall wellbeing, and faith can play a vital role in supporting mental health for Black women. Prayer, meditation, scripture reading, and communal worship can provide comfort, reduce stress, and promote mental wellbeing. At the same time, faith communities can offer support, understanding, and companionship, helping to combat feelings of loneliness or isolation.

It's important to remember that while faith can provide meaningful support for mental health, it does not replace the need for professional mental health support when needed. A holistic approach to mental health integrates faith practices with professional mental health resources, ensuring that Black women have the necessary support for their mental wellbeing.

Faith as a Source of Joy and Fulfillment

In the face of life's challenges, faith can provide a source of joy and fulfillment for Black women. It can offer a sense of purpose, instill a sense of hope, and provide a foundation for ethical living. The joyful moments of faith – whether in personal reflection, communal worship, or acts of service – can provide comfort and happiness.

The intersection of faith and joy underscores the positive and life-affirming aspects of faith. It's a reminder that faith is not just about beliefs and practices, but also about cultivating a deep sense of joy, peace, and fulfillment.

Conclusion: An Ongoing Journey

Exploring the intersections between race and religion is not a finite process but an ongoing journey. As Black women continue to navigate their faith, these intersections will continue to shape, challenge, and enrich their spiritual experiences. This exploration can empower Black women to understand their faith in deeper ways, foster their spiritual growth, and contribute to their communities in meaningful ways.

Faith, Education, and Enlightenment

The intersection of faith and education is another critical consideration for Black women. Understanding religious texts, doctrines, and history can strengthen and deepen their faith, enabling them to engage more profoundly with their religious beliefs and practices. Furthermore, education about different religious perspectives can foster a more inclusive and tolerant worldview.

Educational pursuits within faith are not limited to formal learning environments. They can encompass personal study, participation in study groups, attending seminars or workshops, or even engaging in meaningful conversations about faith. As Black women continue to educate themselves about their faith and the faith of others, they can experience increased enlightenment and understanding.

Faith and Entrepreneurship: Harnessing Faith in Professional Life

Black women who are entrepreneurs often find their faith to be a guiding and stabilizing force in their professional endeavors. Faith can provide strength during challenging times, inspiration for their work, and guidance in making ethical business decisions. The principles derived from faith, such as integrity, compassion, and perseverance, can be instrumental in shaping a successful and fulfilling entrepreneurial journey.

Faith-based entrepreneurship can also involve leveraging business as a platform to express and share faith—for instance, through ethical business practices, faith-based products or services, or community outreach initiatives. By integrating their faith and professional life, Black women can create businesses that reflect their values and contribute positively to their communities.

Faith and Social Media: Digital Spaces for Faith Expression and Community

In the digital age, social media offers new opportunities for expressing faith and fostering online faith communities. Platforms such as Facebook, Instagram, YouTube, and Twitter allow Black women to share their faith experiences, seek spiritual inspiration, and connect with others who share their beliefs.

While online spaces cannot replace the value of in-person community, they can complement it, offering new avenues for connection, learning, and engagement. By navigating these digital spaces with discernment and intention, Black women can enrich their faith experience and contribute to the digital faith community.

Eco-faith: Intersection of Faith and Environmental Stewardship

The connection between faith and environmental stewardship, often referred to as eco-faith, is an area of increasing relevance. Many faith traditions emphasize the importance of caring for creation, recognizing the inherent worth of the natural world. For Black women, exploring the connection between their faith and environmental stewardship can offer a deeper understanding of their responsibility towards the environment.

Eco-faith can involve practical actions such as recycling, advocating for environmental policies, or participating in clean-up efforts, as well as spiritual practices that foster a sense of connection with nature. By engaging with eco-faith, Black women can express their faith in ways that contribute to environmental sustainability and justice.

Concluding Thoughts: An Unfolding Tapestry of Faith

Exploring the intersections of race and religion creates a rich tapestry of experiences, insights, and challenges for Black women. It is an ongoing journey that involves deep personal reflection, community engagement, and continuous learning. As they navigate these intersections, Black women are not just passive recipients of their faith. They are active participants, shaping and being shaped by their faith in ways that are deeply personal, profoundly communal, and innately powerful. This exploration is not just about understanding faith—it's about living it.

Women of the Bible: Lessons and Inspiration

Exploring the stories of women in the Bible can offer significant insights and inspiration for Black women today. Despite the historical and cultural differences, the faith, courage, wisdom, and resilience of these biblical women can provide valuable lessons for modern faith journeys.

Whether it's the audacious faith of Rahab, the strategic wisdom of Esther, or the persevering prayer of Hannah, these stories illuminate different aspects of faith. They demonstrate that faith is not about perfection, but about trust in God, resilience in adversity, and courage to do what is right.

By engaging with these stories, Black women can draw strength and encouragement for their faith journeys. These biblical women serve as reminders that they are part of a long, enduring narrative of faith.

Faith and Feminism: Advocacy for Gender Equality

For many Black women, their faith and their advocacy for gender equality are deeply intertwined. They see their faith not as a barrier to equality, but as a catalyst for it. From a faith perspective, they advocate for the inherent worth and equality of all genders, challenging patriarchal structures and biases within religious and societal contexts.

Faith-based feminism is about reclaiming the egalitarian principles within faith traditions and applying them to advocate for gender equality. It involves challenging oppressive practices, advocating for women's rights and representation, and fostering an inclusive faith community that affirms the equal value of all its members.

Faith and Body Positivity: Embracing Divine Image

The intersection of faith and body positivity is another important consideration. Many faith traditions affirm that humans are made in the divine image, implying an inherent worth and dignity. For Black women, this belief can be a source of body positivity, challenging societal beauty standards and promoting self-acceptance.

Faith-based body positivity involves seeing the body not as an object of societal judgment but as a divine gift. It encourages self-care, gratitude, and respect for the body. By affirming their bodies as a reflection of the divine image, Black women can foster a healthy and positive body image, regardless of societal standards.

Faith, Hope, and Love: The Heart of Faith Experience

At the core of many faith traditions are the virtues of faith, hope, and love. These virtues underpin the faith experience of Black women, guiding their beliefs, shaping their actions, and enriching their spiritual journeys.

Faith is about trust and conviction, holding onto beliefs even in the face of uncertainty. Hope is about expectancy and optimism, looking forward to better times and trusting in divine promises. Love is about compassion and selflessness, caring for others and reflecting divine love in one's actions.

In the intersection of race and religion, these virtues take on a profound significance. They offer strength in adversity, comfort in trials, and motivation to work for justice, equality, and love.

A Multifaceted Faith Journey

The intersection of race and religion in the lives of Black women is a complex, multifaceted journey. It is an exploration of identity, community, resilience, and transformation. It involves not only personal faith experiences but also collective narratives, historical legacies, and shared hopes. Through this journey, Black women continue to shape and be shaped by their faith, contributing to a vibrant and enduring faith tradition.

Music and Worship: A Melody of Faith

Music is a central element of worship in many religious traditions. For Black women, music can be a powerful means of expressing their faith, sharing their spiritual experiences, and connecting with their faith community. Whether through traditional hymns, gospel music, spirituals, or contemporary Christian music, these melodies capture a range of human emotions and experiences from joy and gratitude to sorrow and longing.

The richness of musical worship lies not just in the lyrics but also in the shared experience of singing or listening together. It's a communal act that brings people together, affirming shared beliefs and strengthening community bonds. Through music, Black women can find a voice for their faith, a medium for their worship, and a melody for their spiritual journey.

Art and Faith: Visual Expressions of Spirituality

Art is another powerful medium for expressing faith. It can capture the divine in tangible forms, provoke reflection, and convey spiritual truths in unique and compelling ways. For Black women, engaging with religious art can deepen their understanding of their faith, stimulate their spiritual imagination, and offer new perspectives on familiar faith themes.

Creating religious art is also a spiritual practice in itself. It's a process of contemplation, creativity, and expression that can enrich the faith experience. Whether through painting, sculpture, or other forms of visual art, Black women can explore their faith in ways that are personally meaningful and spiritually rewarding.

Food and Faith: Communal Bonds and Sacred Traditions

Food plays a significant role in many religious traditions. It's often a central part of religious celebrations, rituals, and communal gatherings. For Black women, food and faith intersect in meaningful ways, creating opportunities for community, celebration, and spiritual reflection.

Preparing and sharing meals can be acts of service, hospitality, and fellowship. They can bring people together, fostering a sense of community and shared identity. At the same time, participating in religious rituals involving food can provide a tangible connection to sacred traditions, enhancing the spiritual significance of these practices.

Dance and Faith: Embodied Expressions of Worship

Dance is an embodied form of worship that engages the body, mind, and spirit. It's a means of expressing joy, devotion, and reverence, often in communal settings. For Black women, dance can be a powerful medium for expressing their faith and connecting with their faith community.

Whether in the form of traditional African dances, liturgical dances, or other forms of religious dance, these movements can communicate spiritual truths in a visceral and compelling way. They can create a sense of unity, celebration, and spiritual transcendence, enriching the worship experience.

Faith in Many Forms

Exploring the intersections between race and religion reveals a rich diversity of faith expressions among Black women. From music and art to food and dance, these expressions reflect a faith that is vibrant, diverse, and deeply embedded in their daily lives. It's a reminder that faith is not just a set of beliefs or practices but a lived experience that permeates every aspect of life.

Faith and Family: Nurturing Spiritual Legacy

The intersection of faith and family holds profound significance for Black women. Faith traditions often emphasize the importance of family, recognizing it as a crucial environment for nurturing spiritual growth and transmitting religious heritage. For Black women, their role in the family can encompass spiritual nurturing, prayerful intercession, and moral instruction, among others.

In the context of family, faith becomes an integral part of shared experiences - mealtime prayers, Bible stories at bedtime, holiday traditions, or attending church services together. These moments of shared faith not only strengthen family bonds but also ensure the continuation of spiritual legacy, passing down faith from one generation to the next.

Faith and Community Service: Living Out Faith in Action

For many Black women, faith extends beyond personal spiritual practices and permeates their engagement with their communities. They embody their faith through acts of service, advocating for social justice, supporting those in need, and fostering community development. This active expression of faith in service is a testament to the transformative power of faith to not just uplift individuals but entire communities.

Community service as an expression of faith can take many forms - volunteering at local shelters, mentoring young people, advocating for policy changes, or participating in charity work. Such acts of service reflect the core values of love, compassion, and justice embedded in many faith traditions, serving as practical manifestations of these principles.

Faith and Personal Development: Fostering Inner Growth

The intersection of faith and personal development is another important aspect of the faith journey for Black women. Personal development involves self-awareness, emotional growth, skill development, and achieving personal goals, and faith can significantly contribute to these areas. It can provide moral guidance, foster resilience, promote self-discipline, and instill a sense of purpose and meaning.

Whether through personal reflection, meditation, prayer, or engaging with religious texts, faith-based personal development can lead to increased self-understanding, emotional maturity, and spiritual growth. It's an ongoing journey of learning, growing, and evolving, underpinned by faith.

Faith, A Lifelong Journey

The intersection of race and religion is not a static point but a dynamic, evolving journey for Black women. This journey weaves through various facets of life, shaping and being shaped by personal experiences, community contexts, and societal realities. Through this journey, Black women continue to explore, express, and experience their faith in ways that are deeply personal, profoundly communal, and profoundly empowering. They shape their faith tradition even as they are shaped by it, contributing to its richness, diversity, and resilience.

Faith and Mental Health: The Healing Power of Belief

The correlation between faith and mental health is a topic of growing interest in recent years. Many studies have demonstrated that a strong faith or spiritual life can have positive effects on mental health. For Black women, their faith can be a source of comfort and strength, helping them navigate the challenges of life, provide a sense of purpose, and foster a sense of belonging and community.

Faith practices such as prayer, meditation, and community involvement can also provide coping mechanisms during times of stress or adversity. By offering a framework to understand and cope with life's difficulties, faith can promote resilience and psychological well-being. It's important to note, however, that faith is not a substitute for professional mental health services when they are needed but can serve as a complementary resource.

Faith and Aging: Growing Gracefully in Faith

As Black women grow older, their faith often takes on new dimensions. The process of aging, with its unique challenges and opportunities, can deepen their faith, offering profound insights and spiritual growth. This may involve coming to terms with mortality, cherishing the wisdom that comes with age, or mentoring younger generations in their faith journey.

Senior years can be a time of spiritual enrichment, marked by increased prayer, reflection, and spiritual engagement. The faith community also plays a crucial role in this stage of life, providing social support, meaningful engagement, and a sense of belonging.

Faith and the Young Generation: Nurturing Faith in the Future

The intersection of faith and the young generation is another crucial aspect to consider. Young Black women are navigating their own unique challenges in the context of their faith. This includes carving out their identity, exploring their beliefs, and seeking ways to live out their faith authentically.

Engaging the young generation in faith involves listening to their questions, nurturing their spiritual curiosity, and guiding them in their faith journey. It's about creating inclusive and engaging faith environments that resonate with their experiences and aspirations. By investing in the faith development of the young generation, we are nurturing the future bearers of faith traditions.

Conclusion: The Dynamic Intersection of Race and Religion

The journey of faith for Black women is a multifaceted experience, intersecting with various aspects of life. It's a dynamic process that evolves over time, reflecting personal growth, community changes, and societal shifts. As Black women continue to navigate the intersections of race and religion, they enrich their faith tradition with their unique insights, experiences, and contributions. Their journey is a testament to the transformative power of faith, demonstrating its ability to empower, uplift, and inspire.

Afterword

In the journey of self-care, Black women face unique challenges and experiences that require specific attention and support. This book, "Self-Care Affirmations for Black Women," has been crafted with the intention of empowering and uplifting you on your path to holistic well-being. Throughout its pages, we have explored the importance of self-love, inner strength, emotional well-being, healthy relationships, and balancing personal and professional life.

We have delved into the power of affirmations, recognizing them as transformative tools that can shift our mindset, amplify our self-worth, and guide us towards a more fulfilling life. These affirmations serve as reminders of our inherent strength, resilience, and beauty. They encourage us to embrace our identity and celebrate our journey, knowing that we are deserving of love, care, and success.

By integrating these affirmations into our daily lives, we can cultivate a positive and empowering self-narrative. We can challenge limiting beliefs, release self-doubt, and step into our power with confidence. Through the practices of self-care, self-compassion, and intentional living, we can create a strong foundation for our well-being, nurturing our physical, mental, and emotional health.

In recognizing the importance of nurturing our emotional well-being, we have explored strategies to honor our feelings, navigate stress and anxiety, and cultivate resilience. We have celebrated the power of healthy relationships, learning to set boundaries, communicate effectively, and surround ourselves with individuals who uplift and support us. And we have embraced the art of balance, acknowledging that we can create harmony between our personal and professional lives, nurturing both our passions and responsibilities.

Remember, self-care is not selfish; it is a vital act of self-preservation and self-love. By prioritizing our well-being, we are better equipped to navigate life's challenges, support others, and contribute to our communities. As Black women, we have a unique strength, resilience, and beauty that deserves to be nurtured and celebrated.

As you close this book, carry the wisdom, guidance, and affirmations with you. Embrace the journey of self-care as an ongoing practice, knowing that you are worthy of love, care, and joy. Let the affirmations become your allies, guiding you towards a life of empowerment, authenticity, and fulfillment.

May this book serve as a constant reminder that you are enough, you are deserving, and you are capable of creating a life filled with self-love, abundance, and happiness. Your well-being matters, and your journey of self-care is a powerful testament to your strength, resilience, and beautiful spirit.

Go forth, Black woman, and let your self-care journey unfold. Embrace the power of affirmations, nourish your mind, body, and soul, and continue to shine brightly as a beacon of inspiration and love.

Remember, you are worthy of every care and kindness in the world.

With love and empowerment,
Simone Bello